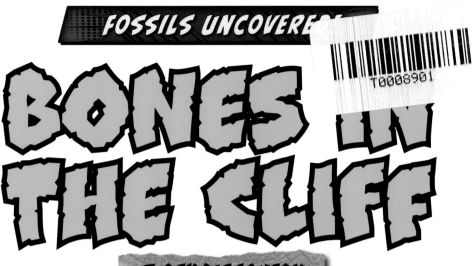

FOSSILS UNCOVERED

BONES IN THE CLIFF

T. REX DISCOVERY

By Sarah Eason
Illustrated by Ludovic Sallé

BEARPORT
PUBLISHING

Minneapolis, Minnesota

BEAR CLAW

Credits: 20b, © Freestyle Images/Shutterstock; 21t, © YuRi Photolife/Shutterstock; 21b, © David Roland/Shutterstock; 22l, © Kriengsak Wiriyakrieng/Shutterstock; 22r, © Microgen/Shutterstock; 23b, © LegART/Shutterstock.

Editor: Jennifer Sanderson
Proofreader: Harriet McGregor
Designer: Paul Myerscough
Picture Researcher: Rachel Blount

DISCLAIMER: This graphic story is a dramatization based on true events. It is intended to give the reader a sense of the narrative rather than a presentation of actual details as they occurred.

Library of Congress Cataloging-in-Publication Data

Names: Eason, Sarah, author. | Salle, Ludovic, 1985- illustrator.
Title: Bones in the cliff : T. rex discovery / by Sarah Eason ; illustrated
  by Ludovic Sallé.
Description: Bear claw books. | Minneapolis. Minnesota : Bearport
  Publishing Company, [2022] | Series: Fossils uncovered! | Includes
  index.
Identifiers: LCCN 2021026686 (print) | LCCN 2021026687 (ebook) | ISBN
  9781636913322 (library binding) | ISBN 9781636913391 (paperback) | ISBN
  9781636913469 (ebook)
Subjects: LCSH: Hendrickson, Sue, 1949---Juvenile literature. |
  Tyrannosaurus rex--South Dakota--Juvenile literature. | Tyrannosaurus
  rex--South Dakota--Comic books, strips, etc. | Dinosaur tracks--South
  Dakota--Juvenile literature. | Paleontological excavations--South
  Dakota--Juvenile literature. | Paleontology--Juvenile literature. |
  Badlands--South Dakota--Juvenile literature.
Classification: LCC QE862.S3 E278 2022 (print) | LCC QE862.S3 (ebook) |
  DDC 567.912/9--dc23
LC record available at https://lccn.loc.gov/2021026686
LC ebook record available at https://lccn.loc.gov/2021026687

For more information, write to Bearport Publishing, 5357 Penn Avenue South, Minneapolis, MN 55419. Printed in the United States of America.

CONTENTS

CHAPTER 1

BONES IN THE BADLANDS

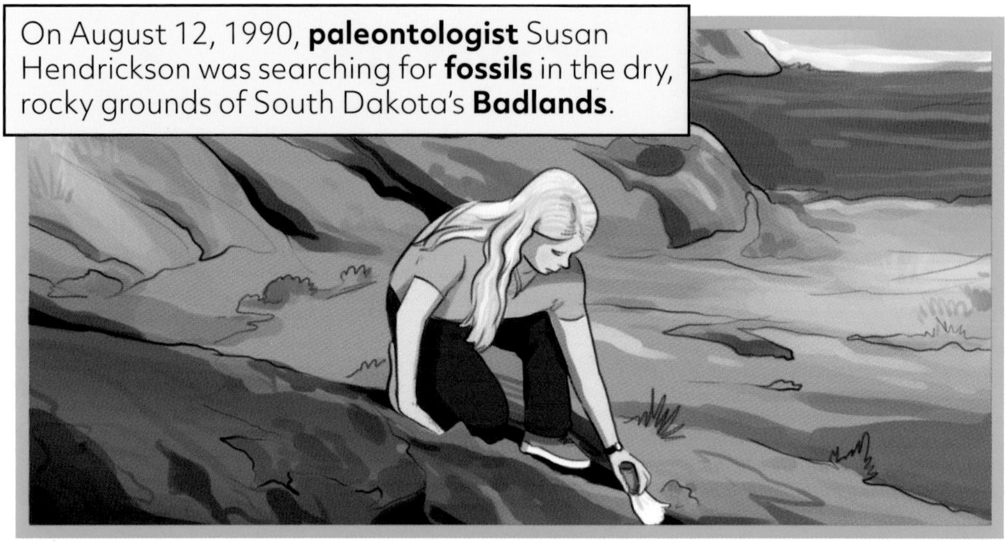
On August 12, 1990, **paleontologist** Susan Hendrickson was searching for **fossils** in the dry, rocky grounds of South Dakota's **Badlands**.

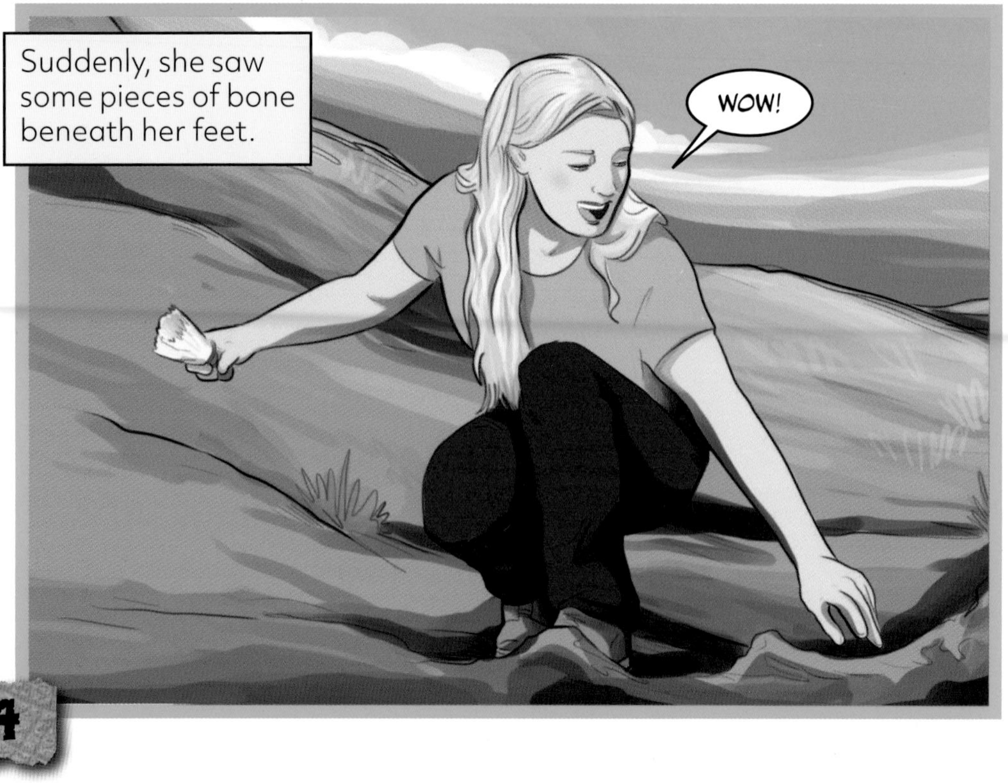
Suddenly, she saw some pieces of bone beneath her feet.
WOW!

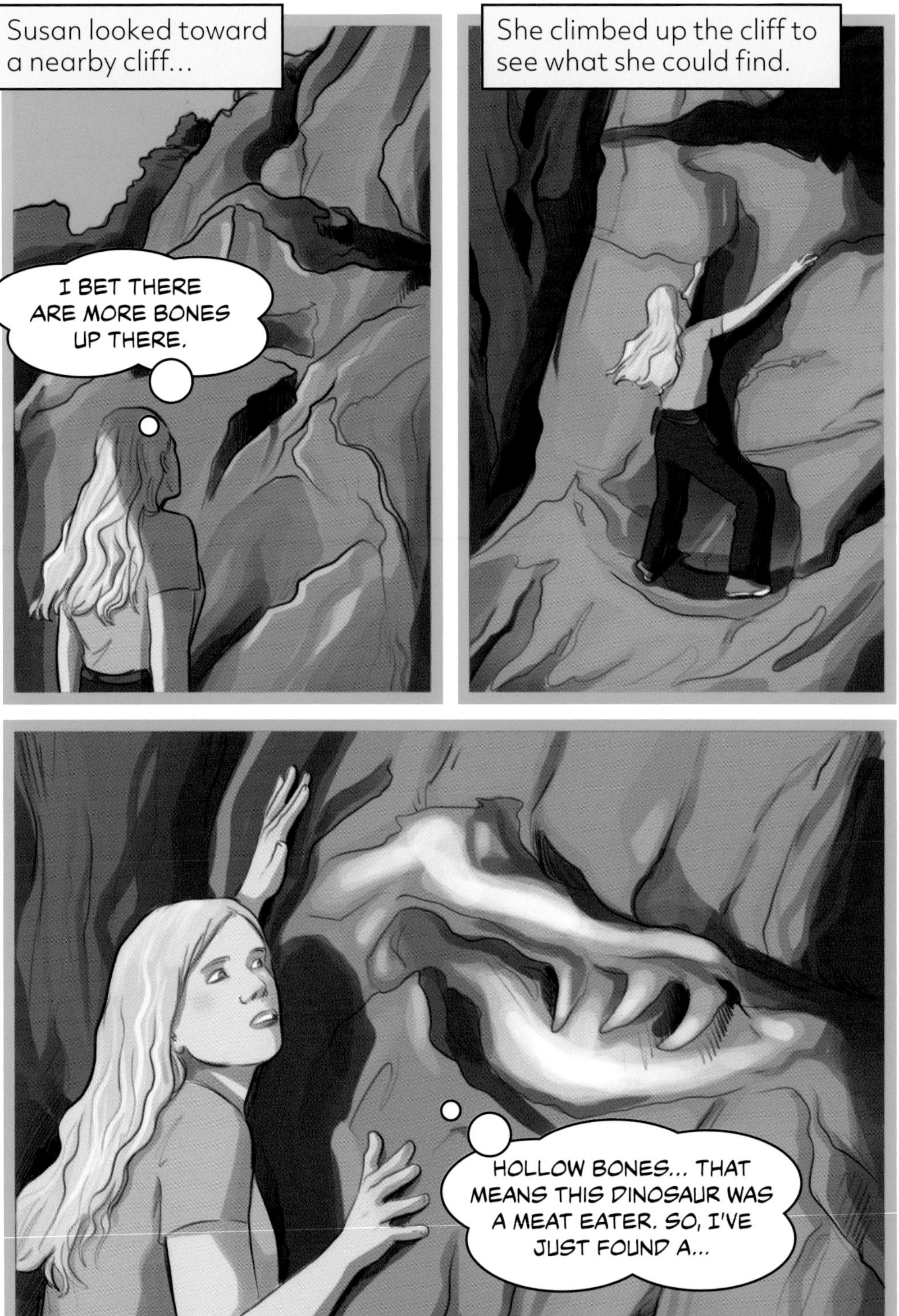
Susan looked toward a nearby cliff...
I BET THERE ARE MORE BONES UP THERE.
She climbed up the cliff to see what she could find.
HOLLOW BONES... THAT MEANS THIS DINOSAUR WAS A MEAT EATER. SO, I'VE JUST FOUND A...

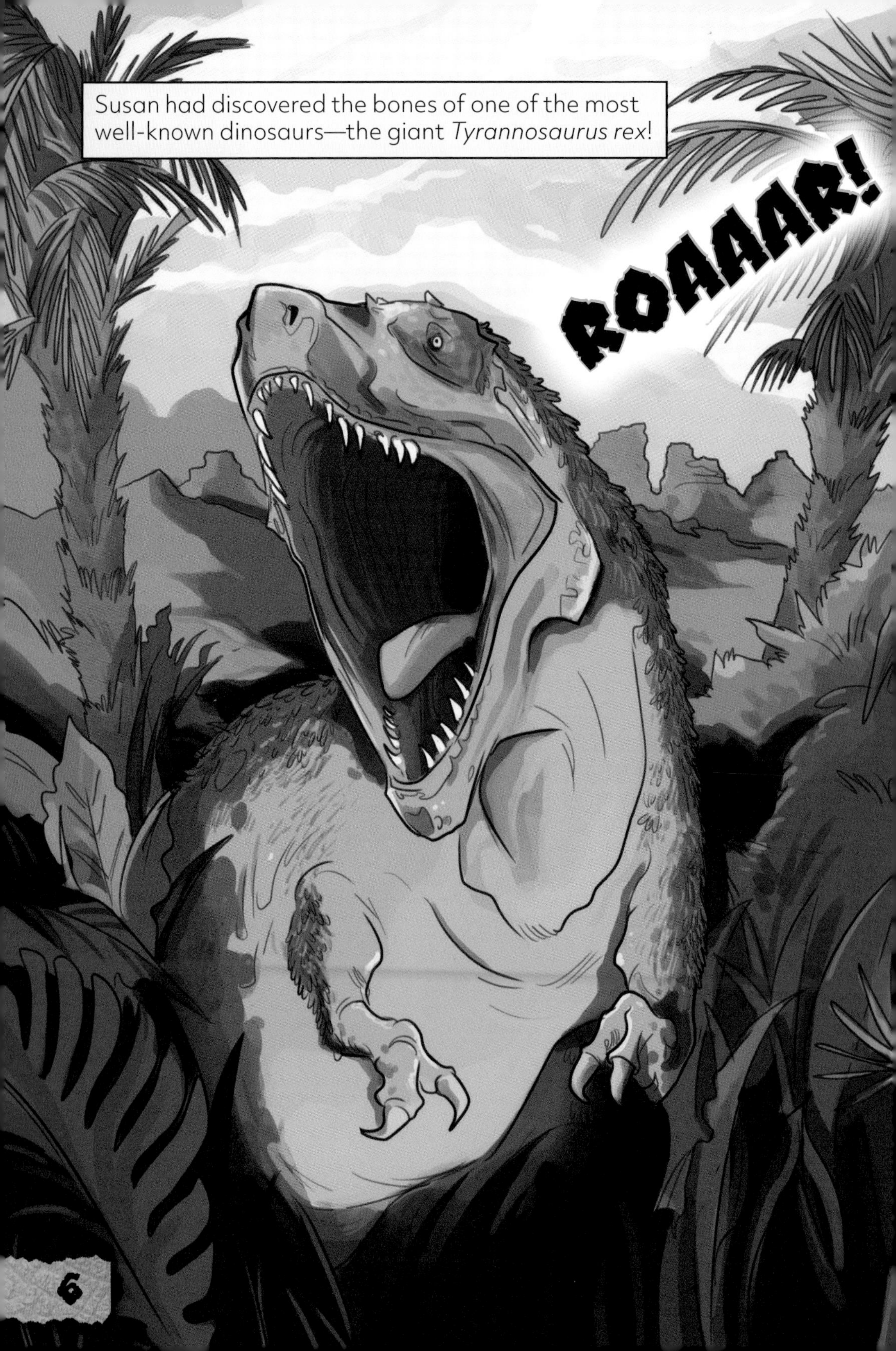
Susan had discovered the bones of one of the most well-known dinosaurs—the giant *Tyrannosaurus rex*!
ROAAAR!

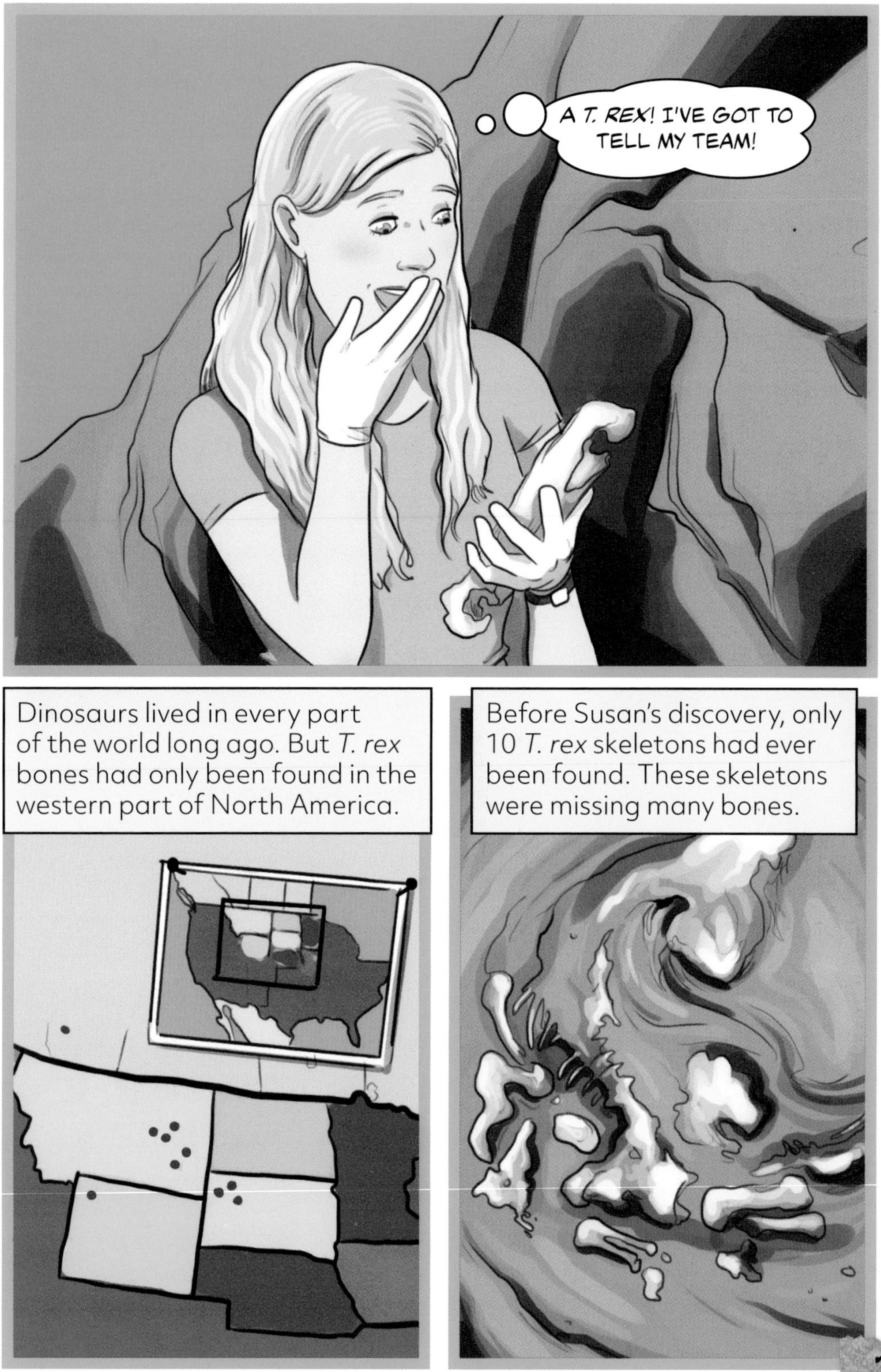
A *T. REX*! I'VE GOT TO TELL MY TEAM!
Dinosaurs lived in every part of the world long ago. But *T. rex* bones had only been found in the western part of North America.
Before Susan's discovery, only 10 *T. rex* skeletons had ever been found. These skeletons were missing many bones.

CHAPTER 2

A DINOSAUR GRAVEYARD

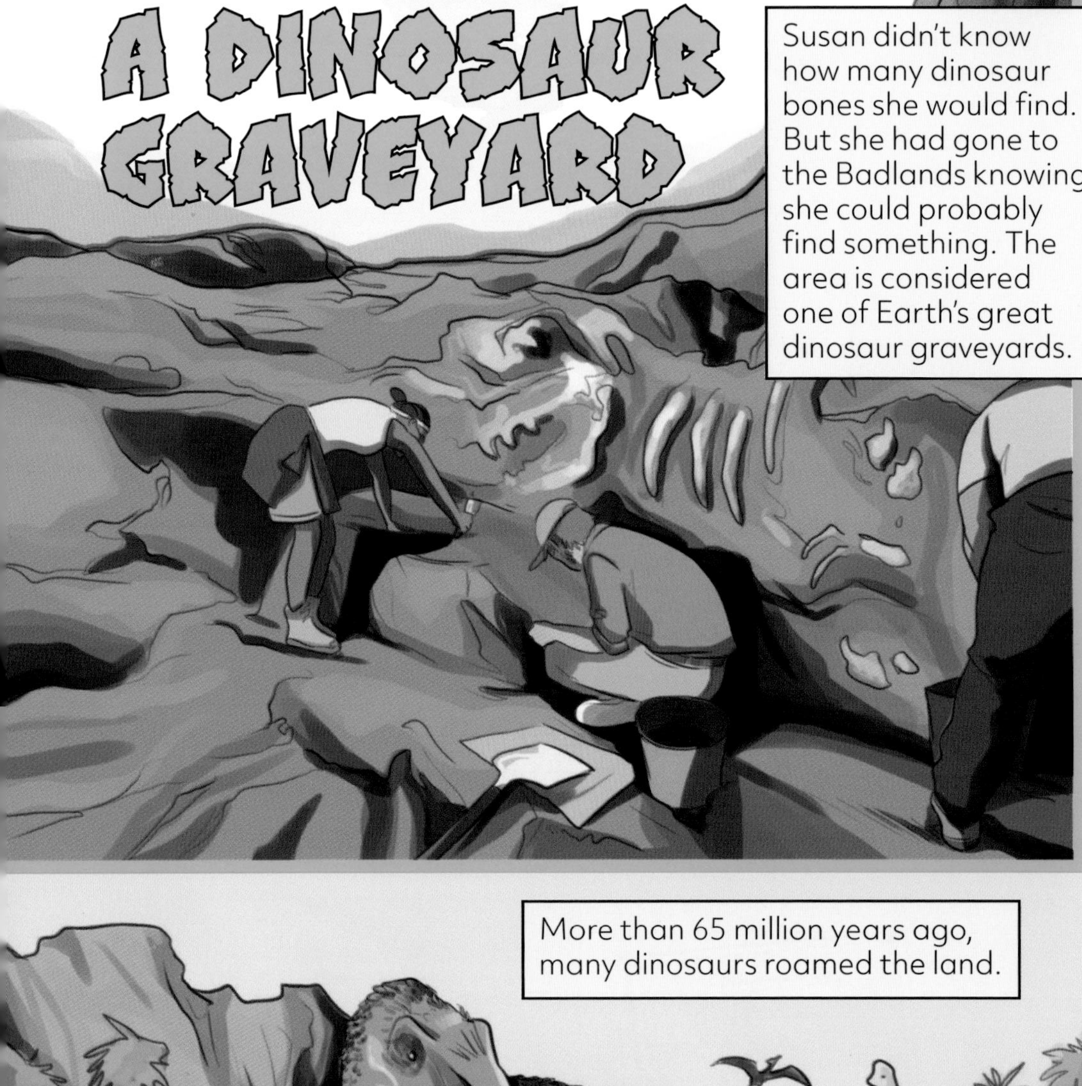
Susan didn't know how many dinosaur bones she would find. But she had gone to the Badlands knowing she could probably find something. The area is considered one of Earth's great dinosaur graveyards.

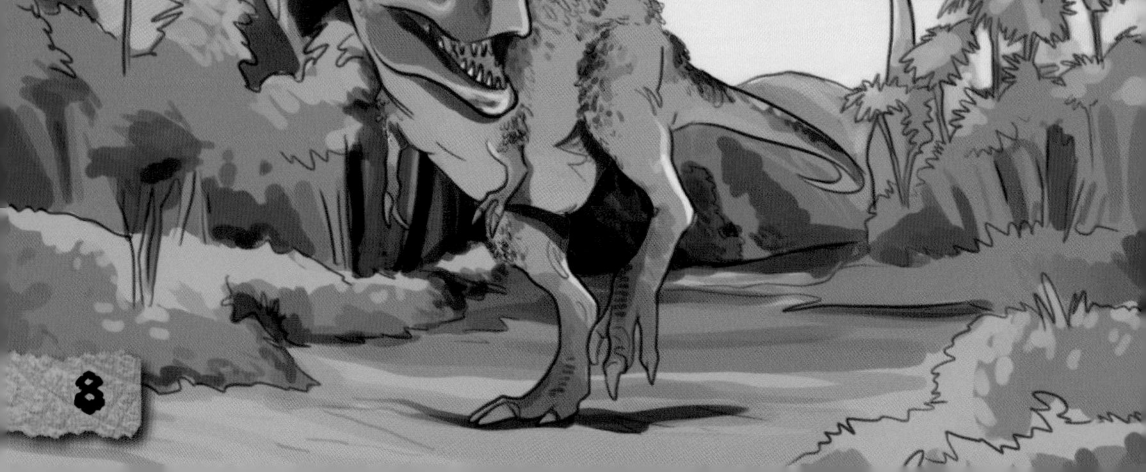
More than 65 million years ago, many dinosaurs roamed the land.

Some dinosaur bones remained as fossils. How?
After a dinosaur died, its soft body parts rotted away.
The hard parts, such as teeth and bones, were left.

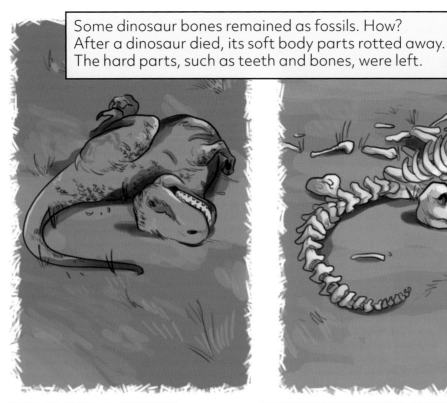

Then, layers of sand and mud covered the skeleton and teeth.

Over millions of years, **minerals** slowly got into the bones and teeth, turning them into fossils.

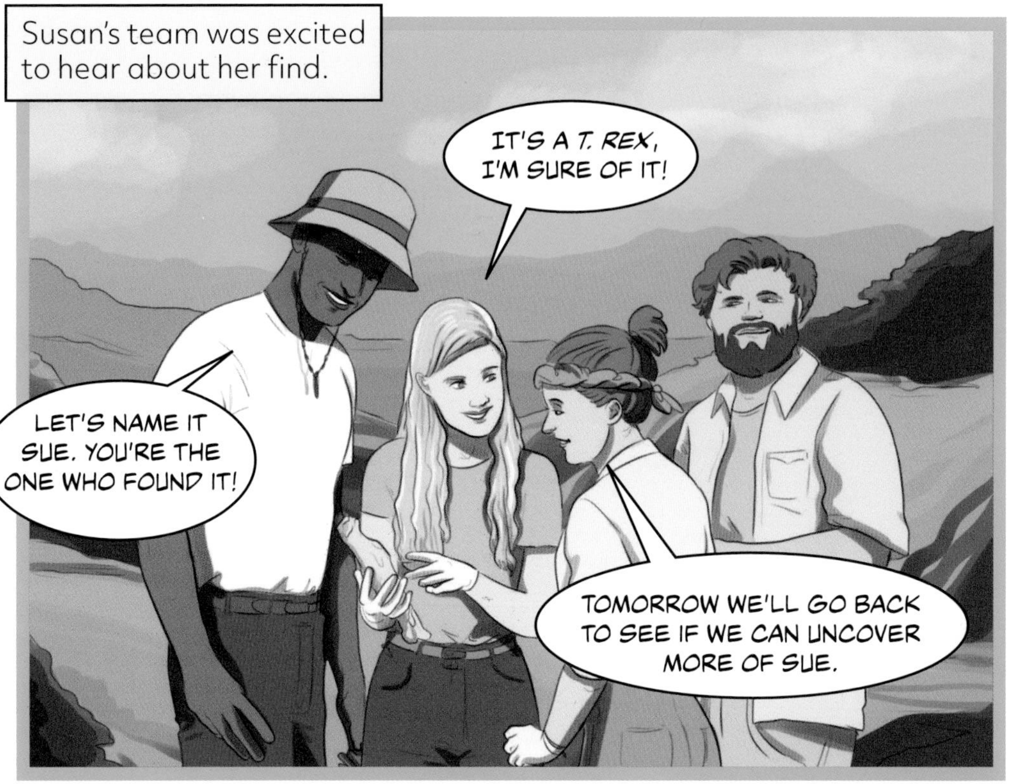
Susan's team was excited to hear about her find.
IT'S A *T. REX*, I'M SURE OF IT!
LET'S NAME IT SUE. YOU'RE THE ONE WHO FOUND IT!
TOMORROW WE'LL GO BACK TO SEE IF WE CAN UNCOVER MORE OF SUE.

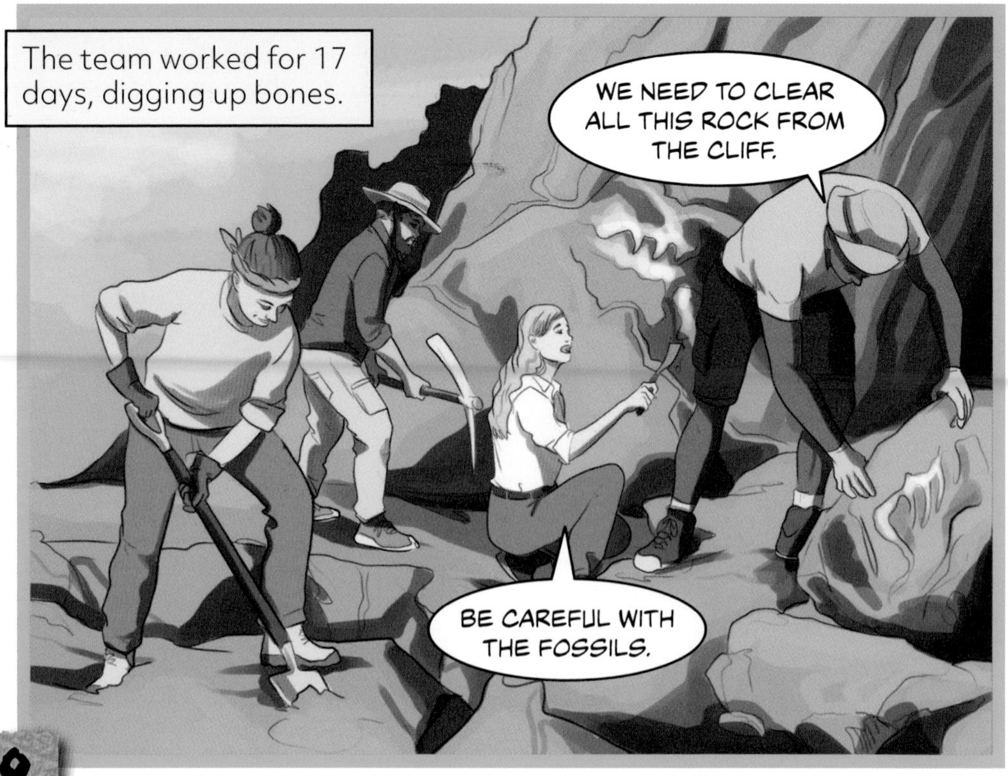
The team worked for 17 days, digging up bones.
WE NEED TO CLEAR ALL THIS ROCK FROM THE CLIFF.
BE CAREFUL WITH THE FOSSILS.

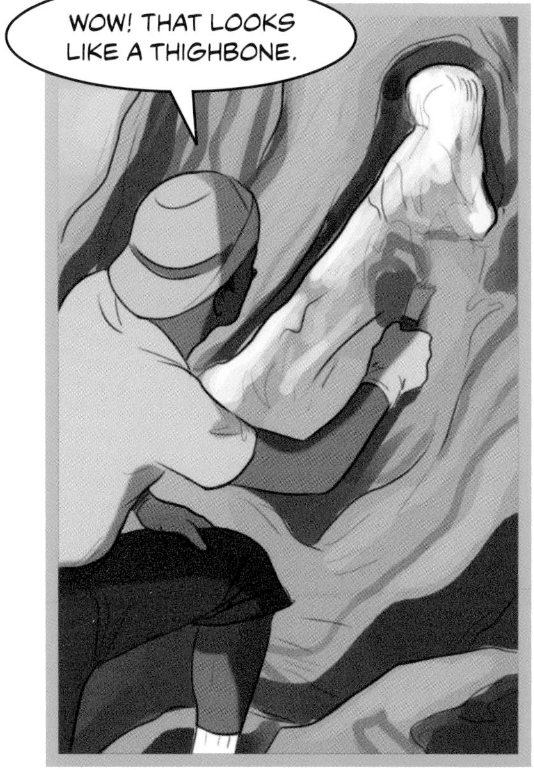
WOW! THAT LOOKS LIKE A THIGHBONE.

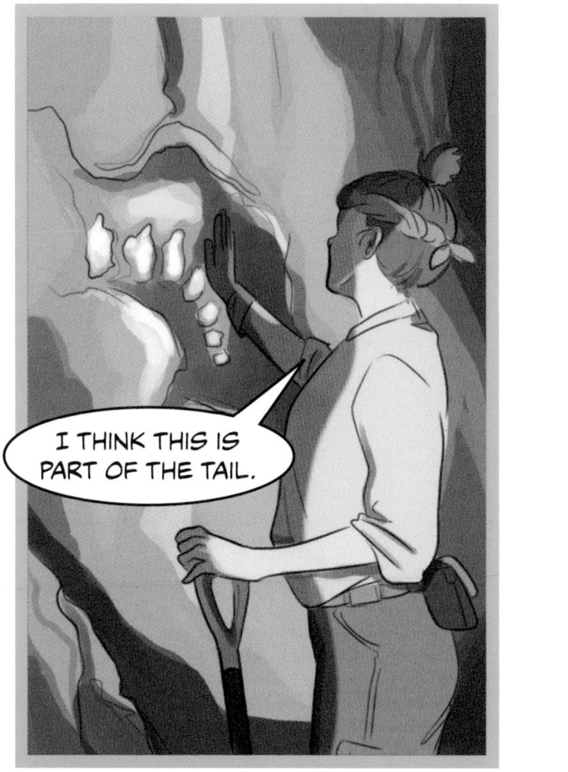
I THINK THIS IS PART OF THE TAIL.

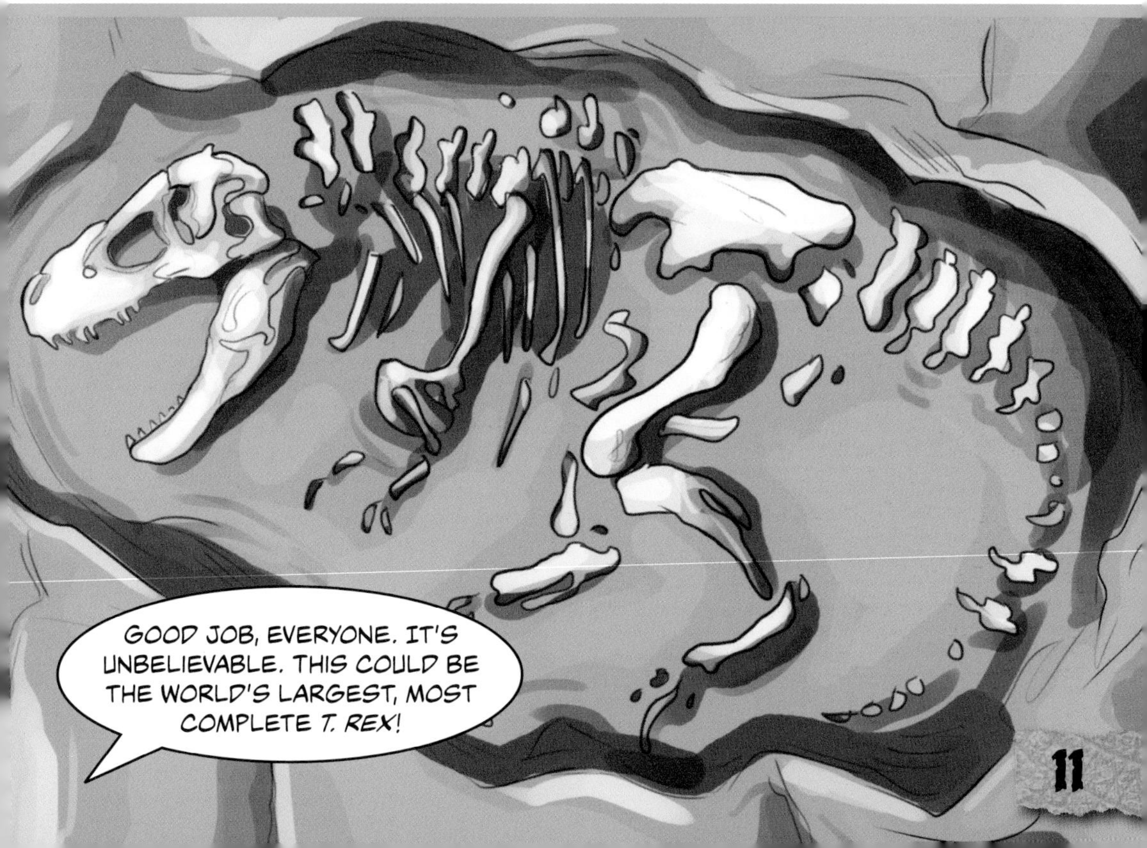
GOOD JOB, EVERYONE. IT'S UNBELIEVABLE. THIS COULD BE THE WORLD'S LARGEST, MOST COMPLETE *T. REX*!

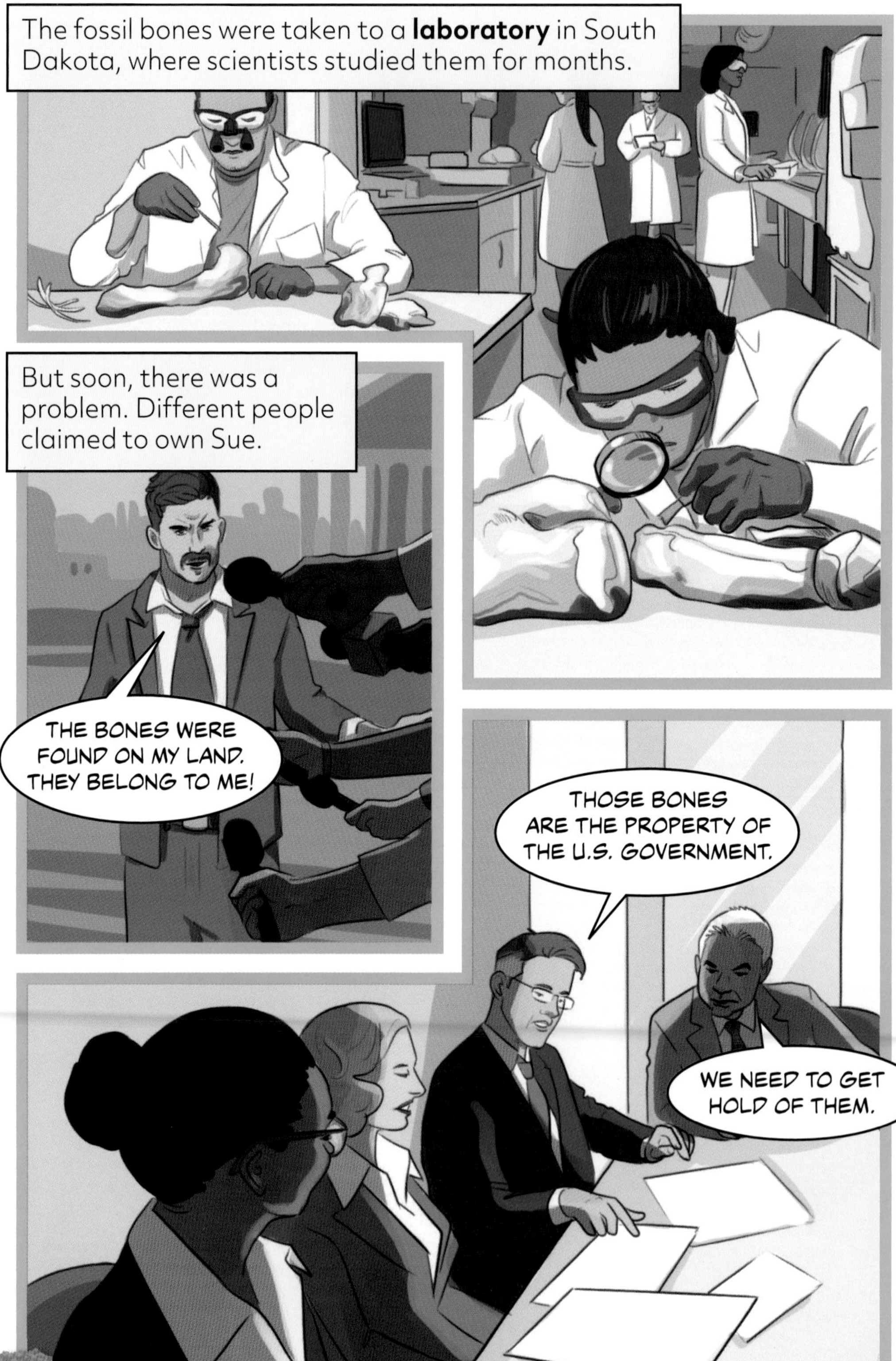
The fossil bones were taken to a **laboratory** in South Dakota, where scientists studied them for months.
But soon, there was a problem. Different people claimed to own Sue.
THE BONES WERE FOUND ON MY LAND. THEY BELONG TO ME!
THOSE BONES ARE THE PROPERTY OF THE U.S. GOVERNMENT.
WE NEED TO GET HOLD OF THEM.

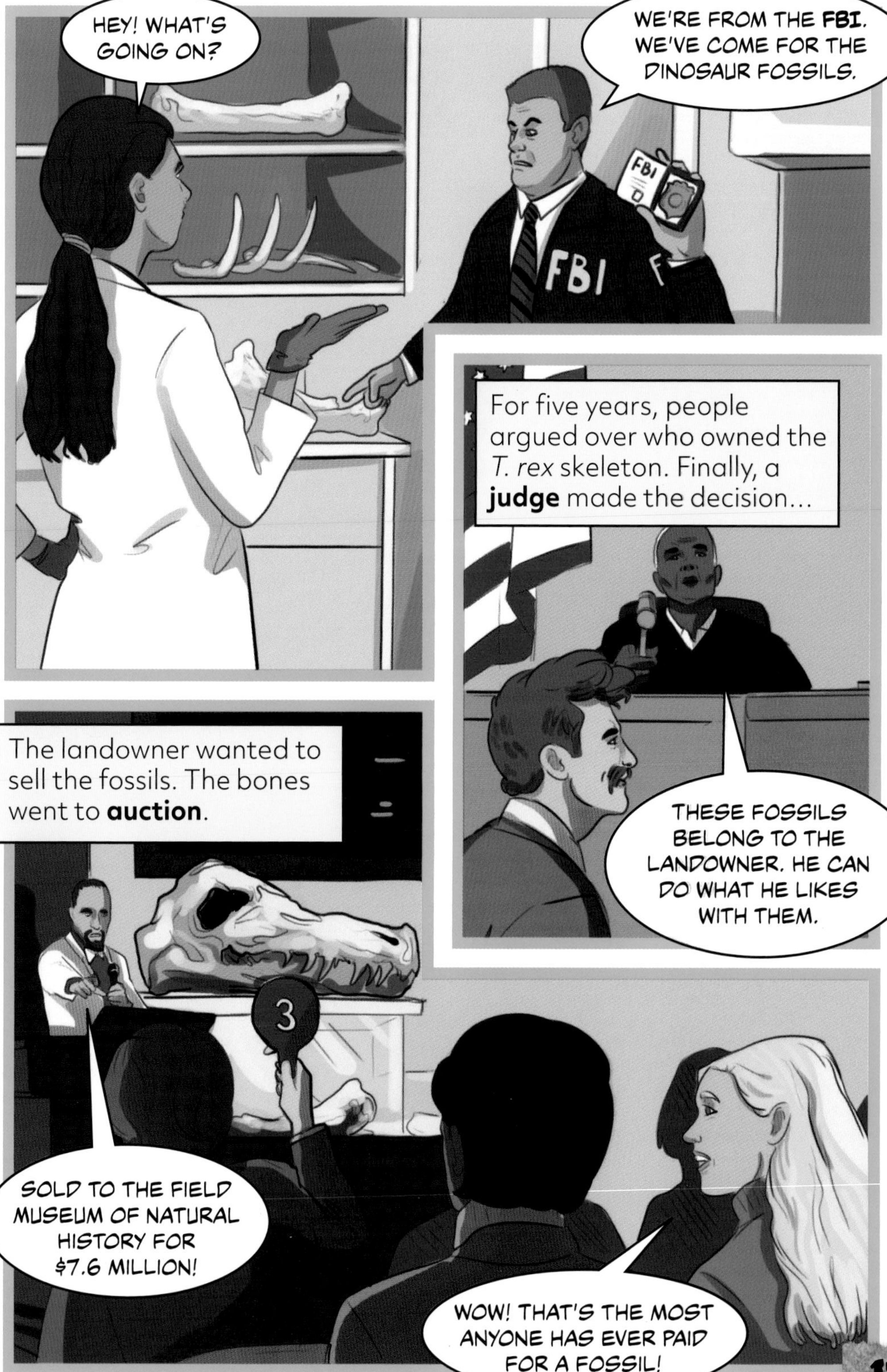
HEY! WHAT'S GOING ON?
WE'RE FROM THE **FBI**. WE'VE COME FOR THE DINOSAUR FOSSILS.
FBI
For five years, people argued over who owned the *T. rex* skeleton. Finally, a **judge** made the decision...
THESE FOSSILS BELONG TO THE LANDOWNER. HE CAN DO WHAT HE LIKES WITH THEM.
The landowner wanted to sell the fossils. The bones went to **auction**.
3
SOLD TO THE FIELD MUSEUM OF NATURAL HISTORY FOR $7.6 MILLION!
WOW! THAT'S THE MOST ANYONE HAS EVER PAID FOR A FOSSIL!

CHAPTER 3

SUE, THE STAR!

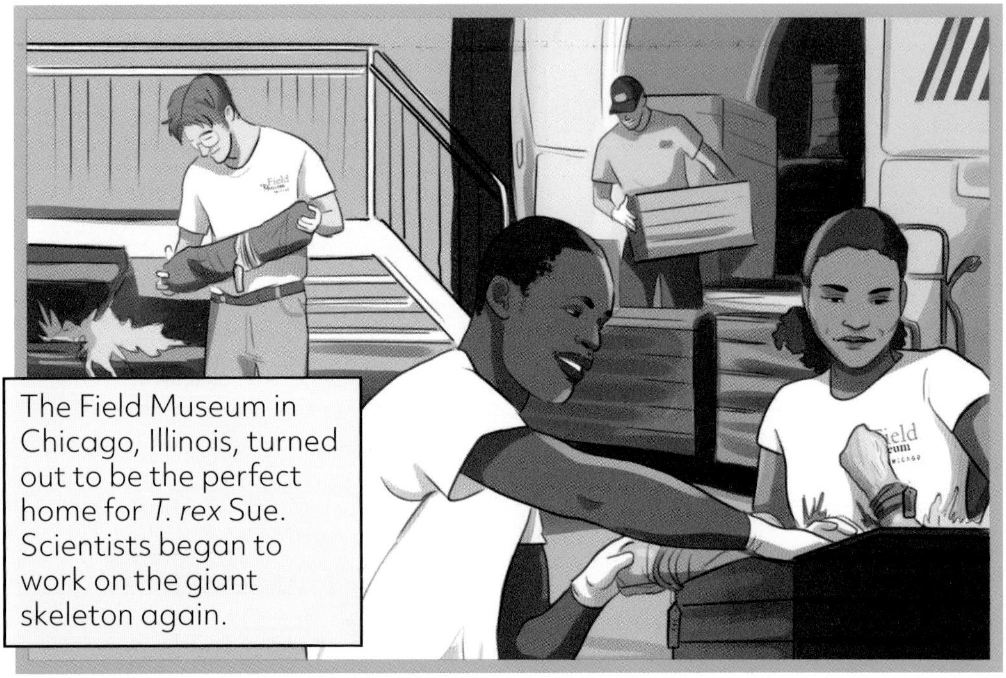

The Field Museum in Chicago, Illinois, turned out to be the perfect home for *T. rex* Sue. Scientists began to work on the giant skeleton again.

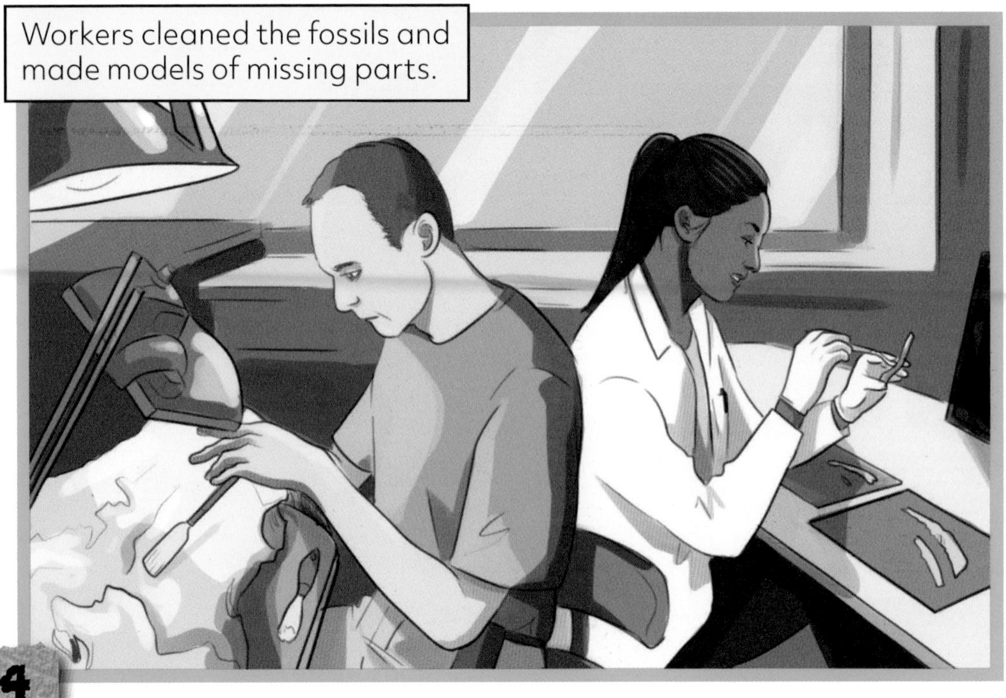

Workers cleaned the fossils and made models of missing parts.

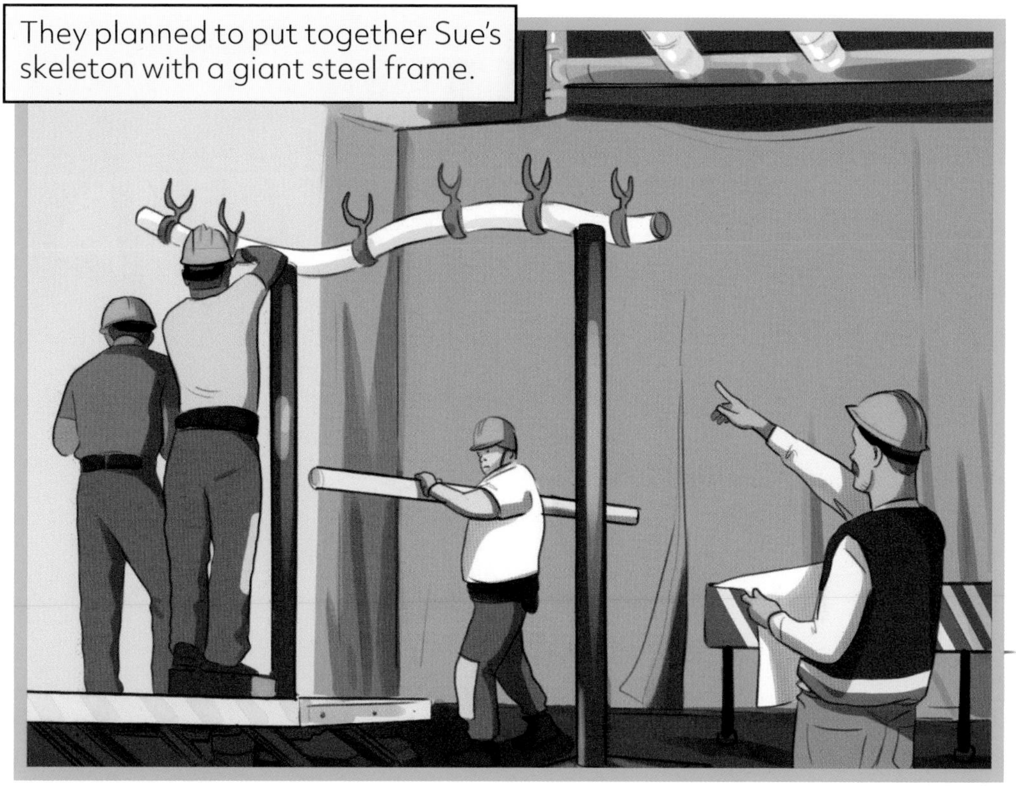
They planned to put together Sue's skeleton with a giant steel frame.

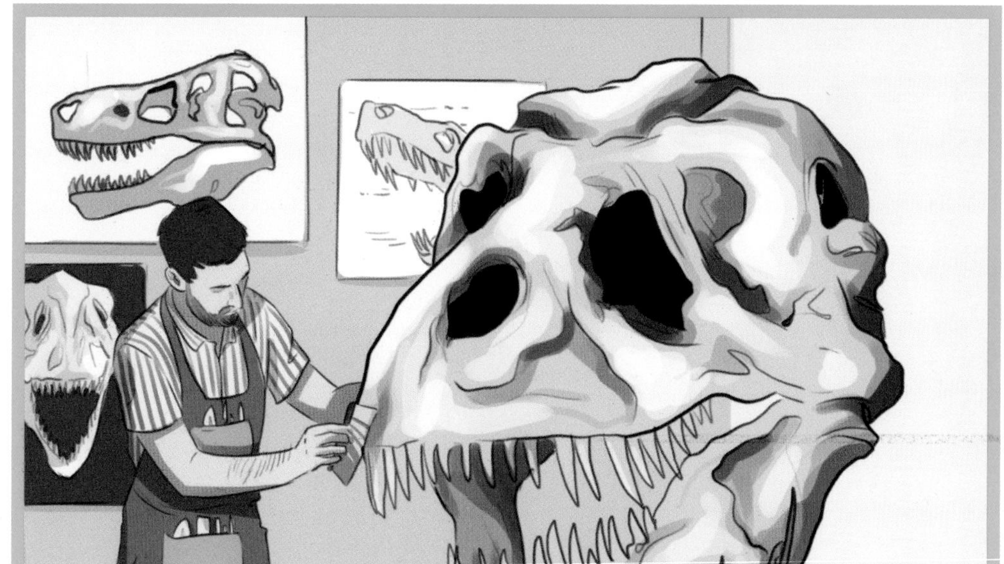
But the skull was too heavy for the frame. So, they made a model of it, too.

Finally, the *T. rex* bones were put together...

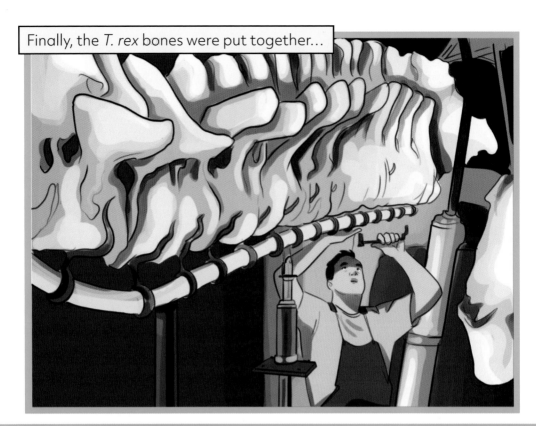

...and the model of Sue's skull was attached.

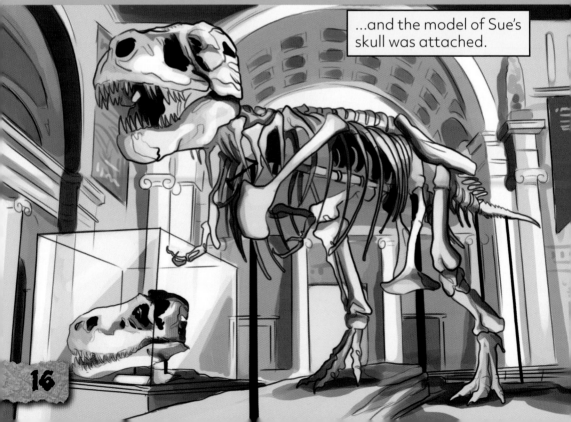

Once Sue had been pieced together, experts could continue to learn more about the *T. rex*.

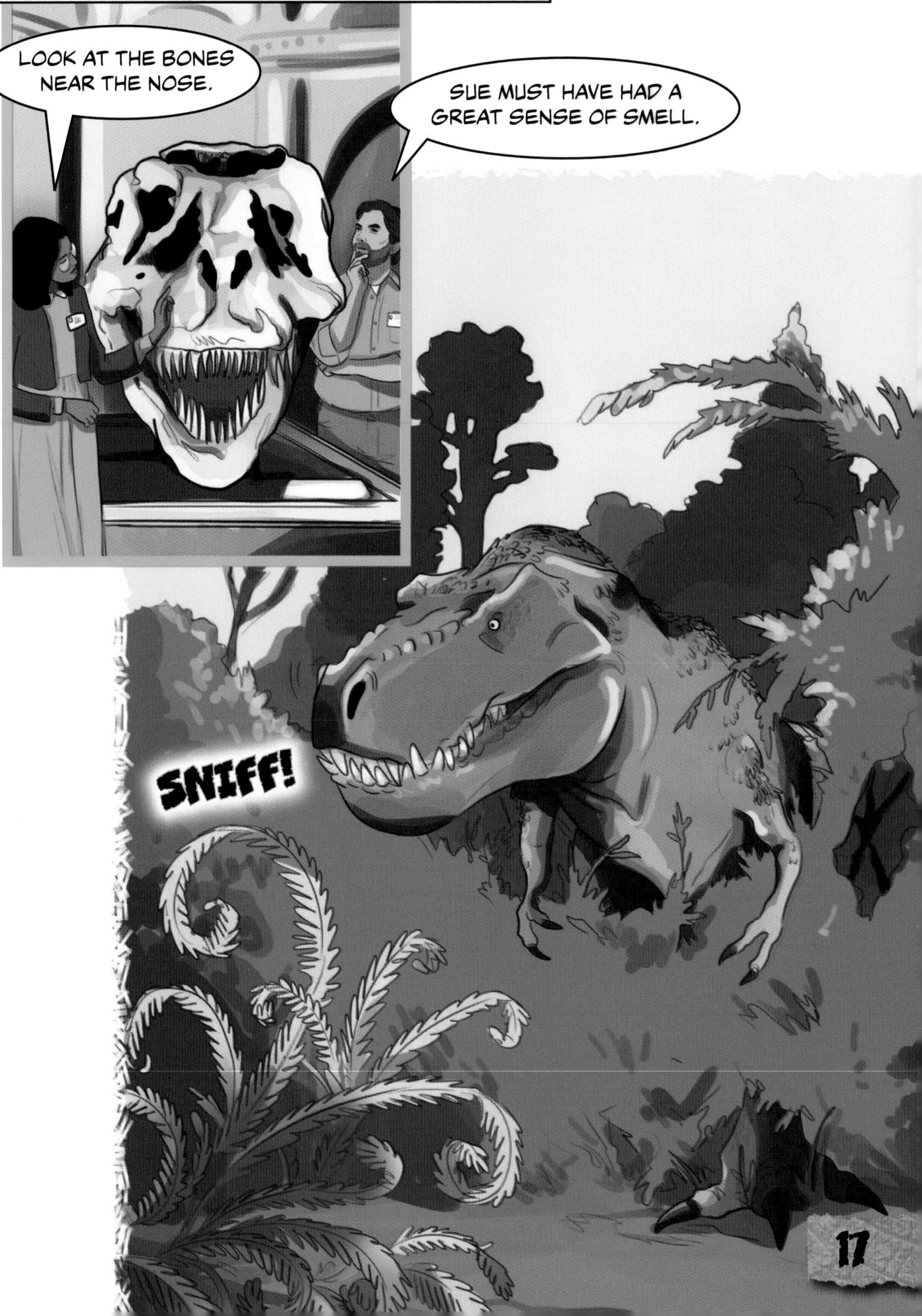

LOOK AT THE BONES NEAR THE NOSE.
SUE MUST HAVE HAD A GREAT SENSE OF SMELL.
SNIFF!

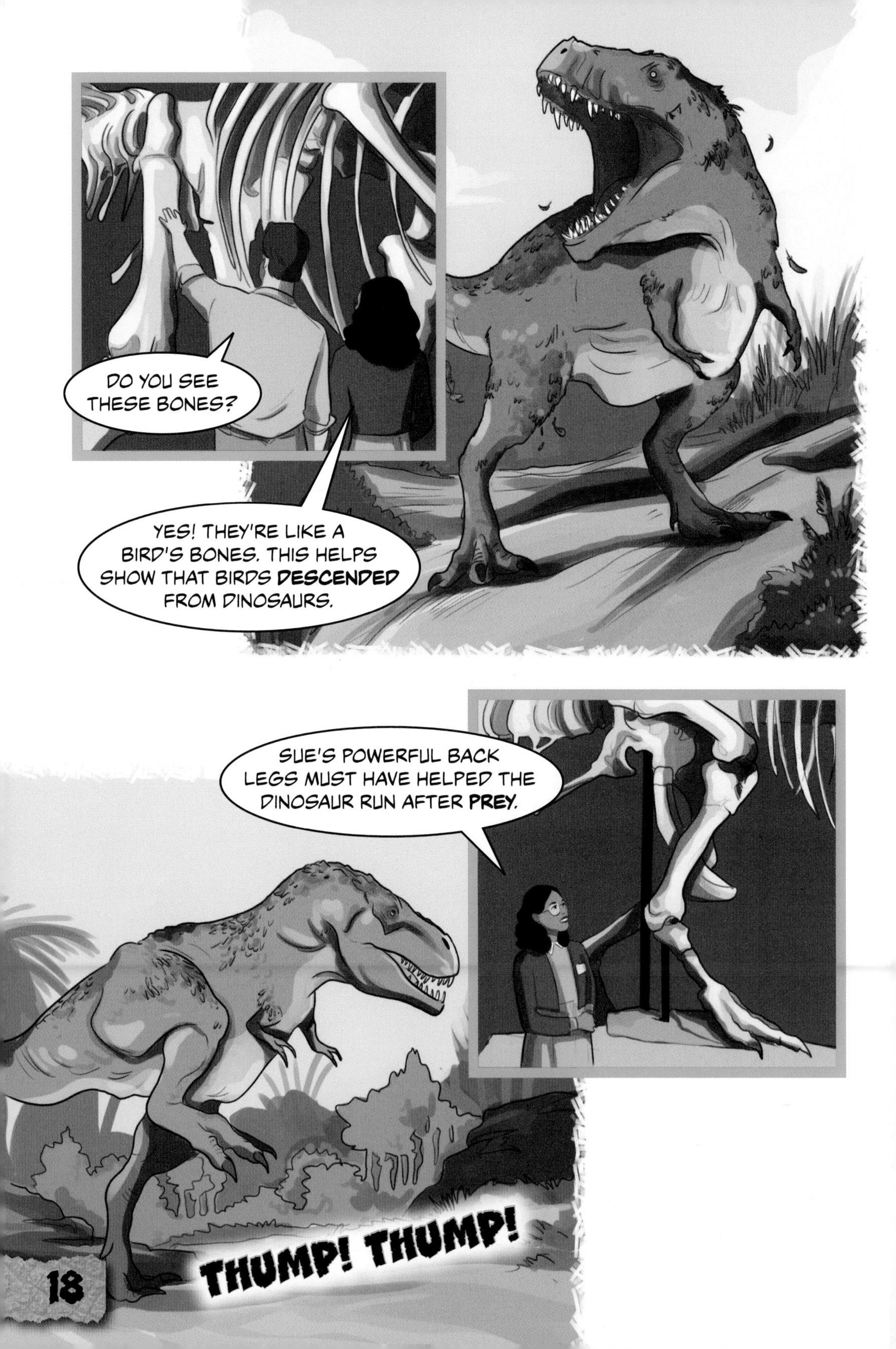

DO YOU SEE THESE BONES?
YES! THEY'RE LIKE A BIRD'S BONES. THIS HELPS SHOW THAT BIRDS **DESCENDED** FROM DINOSAURS.
SUE'S POWERFUL BACK LEGS MUST HAVE HELPED THE DINOSAUR RUN AFTER **PREY**.
THUMP! THUMP!

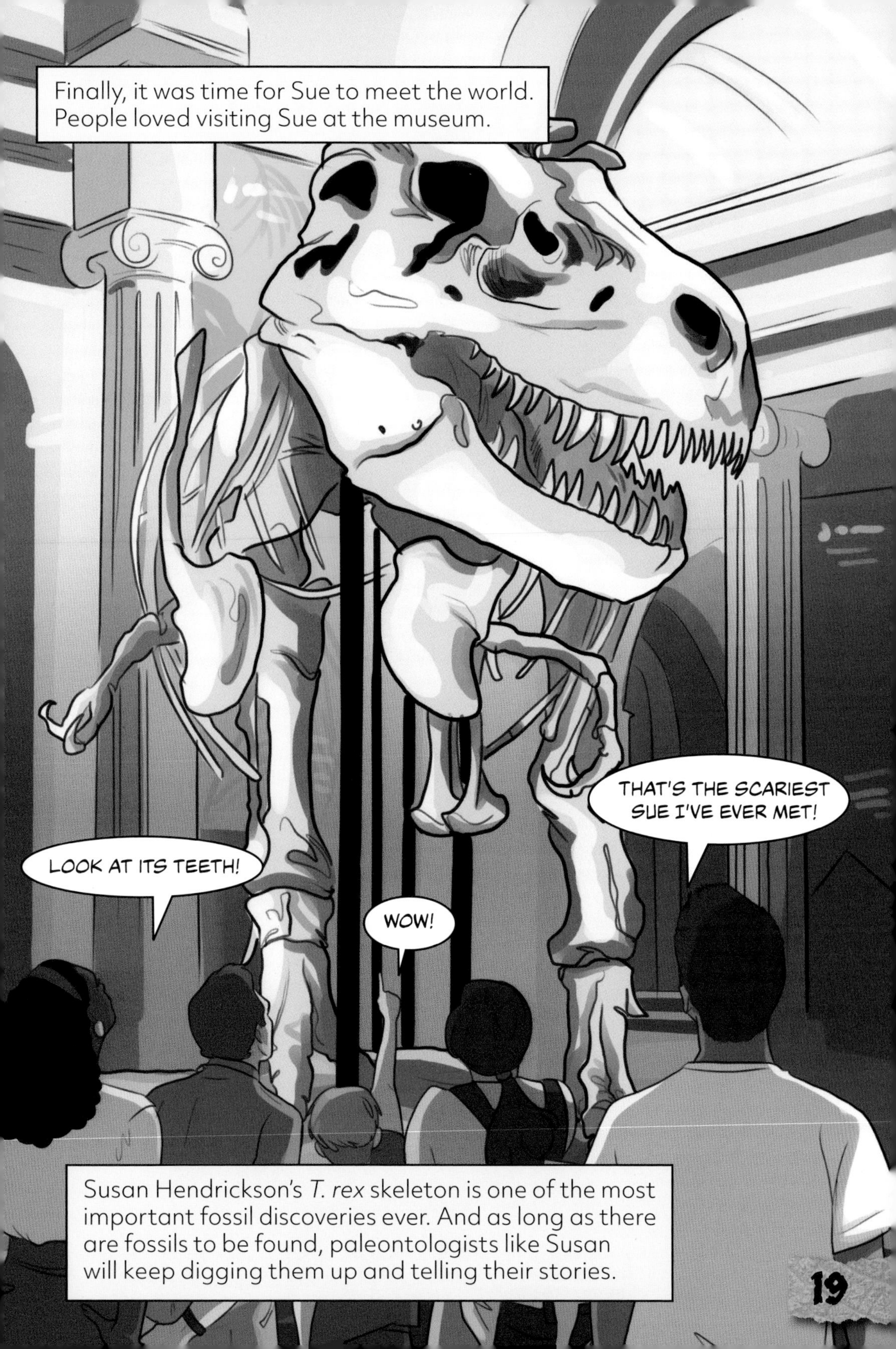
Finally, it was time for Sue to meet the world. People loved visiting Sue at the museum.
LOOK AT ITS TEETH!
WOW!
THAT'S THE SCARIEST SUE I'VE EVER MET!
Susan Hendrickson's *T. rex* skeleton is one of the most important fossil discoveries ever. And as long as there are fossils to be found, paleontologists like Susan will keep digging them up and telling their stories.

Who Lived with *T. rex*?

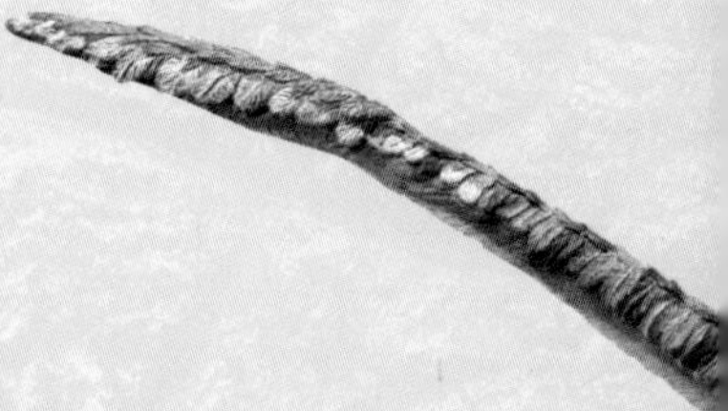

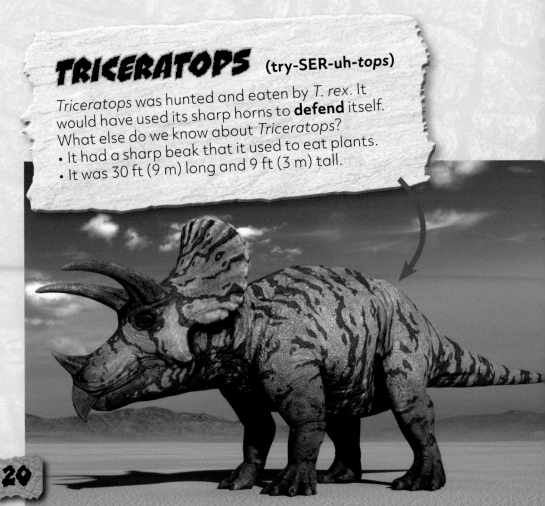

Dinosaurs lived on Earth for about 150 million years. Scientists divide the time in which the dinosaurs lived into three periods—the Triassic period (252 to 201 million years ago), the Jurassic period (201 to 145 million years ago), and the Cretaceous period (145 to 66 million years ago).

T. rex lived near the end of the Cretaceous period. This meat eater was bigger than most other dinosaurs at that time. It was 46 feet (14 m) long and 21 ft (6.5 m) tall when standing upright. Here are three dinosaurs that lived alongside *T. rex*.

TRICERATOPS **(try-SER-uh-*tops*)**

Triceratops was hunted and eaten by *T. rex*. It would have used its sharp horns to **defend** itself. What else do we know about *Triceratops*?

- It had a sharp beak that it used to eat plants.
- It was 30 ft (9 m) long and 9 ft (3 m) tall.

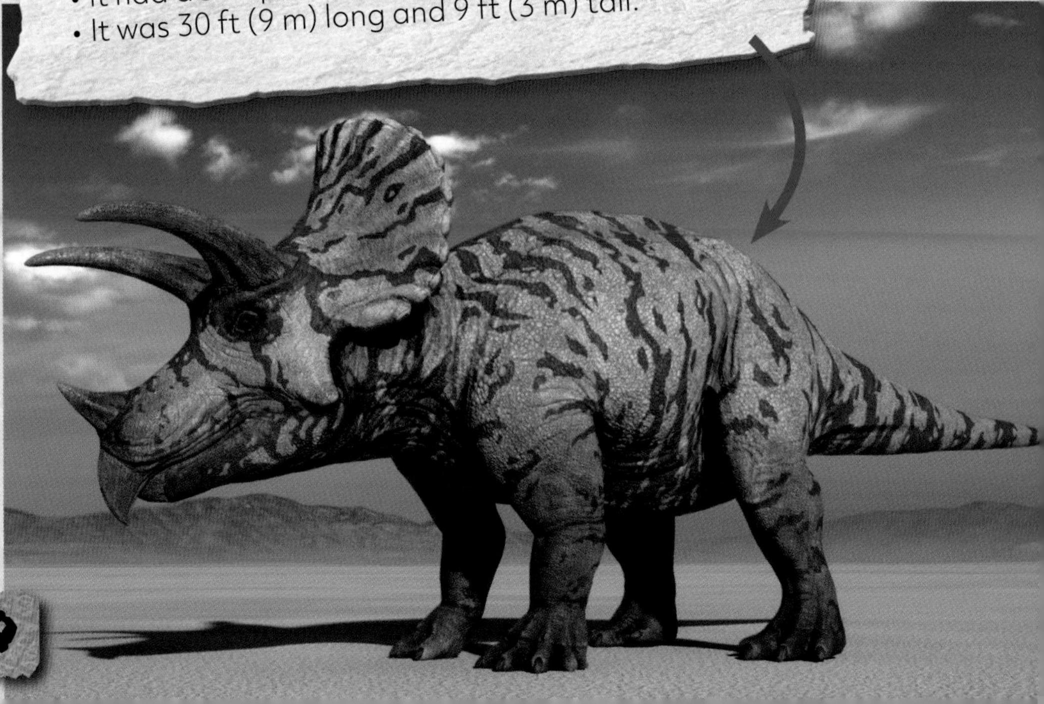

TROODON (TROH-oh-don)

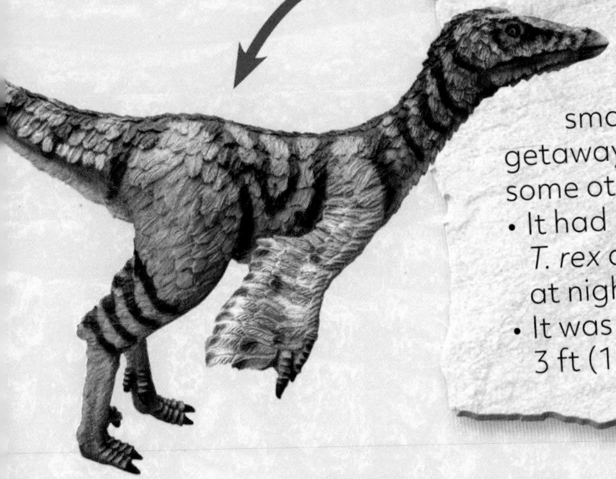

This meat eater was faster and probably a lot smarter than *T. rex*. It was also much smaller and would make a quick getaway if *T. rex* came near. What are some other facts about *Troodon*?

- It had much better sight than *T. rex* and could probably see well at night.
- It was 6 to 11 ft (2 to 3 m) long and 3 ft (1 m) tall.

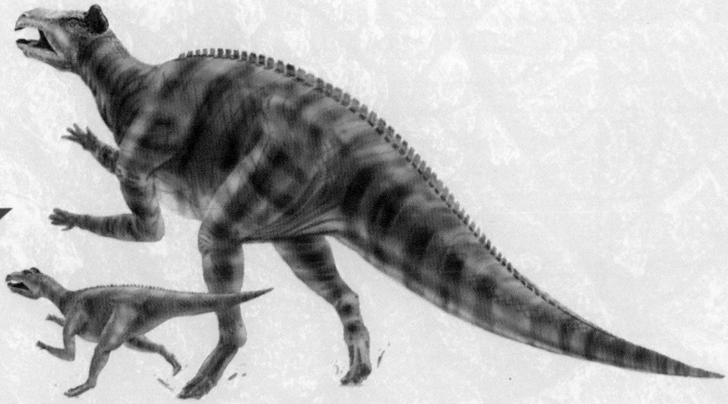

EDMONTOSAURUS

(ed-mon-toh-SOR-uhss)

This plant eater was probably one of *T. rex*'s regular meals. What else have we learned about *Edmontosaurus*?

- It belonged to a group of dinosaurs known as the duckbills, because of their rounded, toothless beaks.
- It was 42 ft (13 m) long and almost as tall as *T. rex*.

What Is Paleontology?

Paleontology is the study of fossils, which are what is left of things that lived millions of years ago. Fossils are found in rock. Paleontologists use special tools to carefully remove the fossils from the rock so they can study them. By studying fossils, paleontologists can figure out where a plant or animal lived, what it looked like, and how it lived.

SOMETIMES PALEONTOLOGISTS STUDY FOSSILS IN LABS. THERE, THEY CAN USE MORE TOOLS TO LEARN ABOUT ANCIENT PLANTS AND ANIMALS.

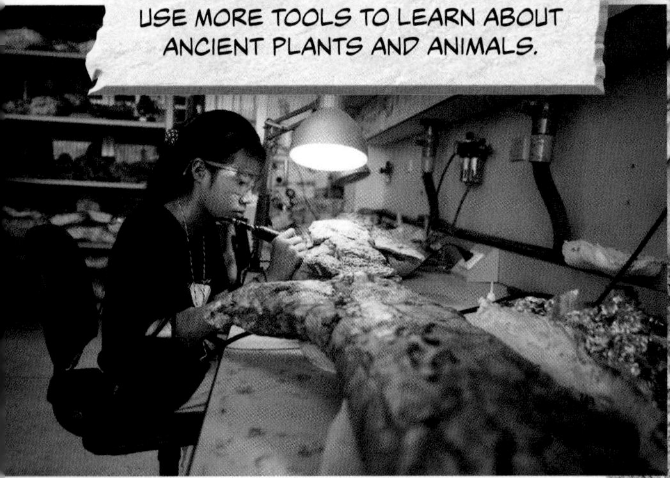

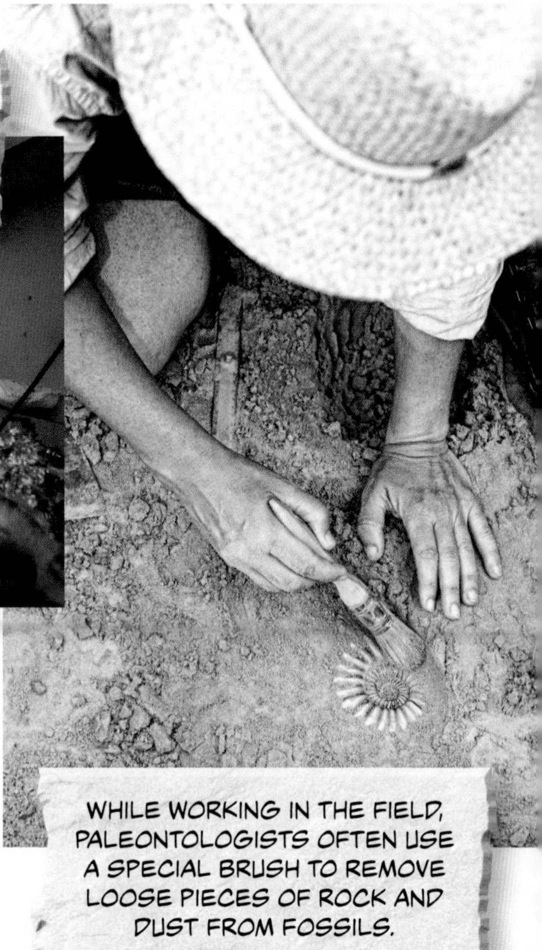

Fossils can show how living things changed over time, too. Paleontologists can use fossils to find out what happened to an **environment** in the past and how living things **adapted** to the changes.

WHILE WORKING IN THE FIELD, PALEONTOLOGISTS OFTEN USE A SPECIAL BRUSH TO REMOVE LOOSE PIECES OF ROCK AND DUST FROM FOSSILS.

Glossary

adapted changed in order to handle new conditions

auction a sale at which something is sold to the person who offers the highest price for it

Badlands an area in South Dakota with rocks that have been made into unusual shapes by strong wind and rain

defend to protect against an attacker

descended came from something that lived long ago

environment the conditions that surround a living thing

FBI Federal Bureau of Investigation; a part of the U.S. government that looks into crimes

fossils the hardened remains of things that lived long ago

judge a person who decides the outcome of cases in court

laboratory a place in which scientists study

minerals solid substances found in nature

paleontologist a scientist who studies fossils to find out about life in the past

prey animals that are hunted and eaten by other animals

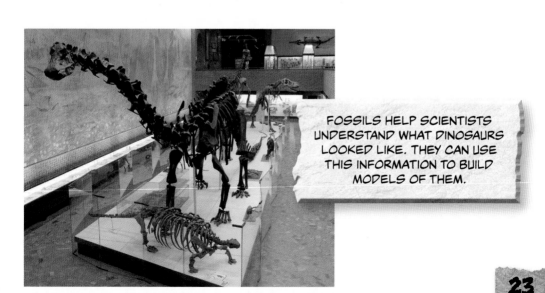

FOSSILS HELP SCIENTISTS UNDERSTAND WHAT DINOSAURS LOOKED LIKE. THEY CAN USE THIS INFORMATION TO BUILD MODELS OF THEM.

Index

Read More

Eason, Sarah. *Bones in the Badlands: Albertosaurus Discovery (Fossils Uncovered!)*. Minneapolis: Bearport Publishing, 2022.

Sabelko, Rebecca. *Tyrannosaurus Rex (Epic: The World of Dinosaurs)*. Minneapolis: Bellwether Media, 2020.

Waxman, Laura Hamilton. *Discovering Tyrannosaurus Rex (Sequence Dinosaurs)*. Mankato, MN: Amicus, 2019.

Learn More Online

1. Go to **www.factsurfer.com** or scan the QR code below.
2. Enter "**Bones Cliff**" into the search box.
3. Click on the cover of this book to see a list of websites.